PRAISE GOD!
JESUS IS BORN!

D1715171

ABINGDON PRESS
NASHVILLE

PRAISE GOD! JESUS IS BORN!

ISBN 978-0-687-49001-1

07 08 09 10 11 12 13 14 15—10 9 8 7 6 5 4 3 2
Manufactured in the United States of America

CONTENTS

THE LIGHT COMES
by LeeDell Stickler
John 1:1-16

Group 1: In the beginning was the Word,

Group 2: and the Word was with God,

All: and the Word was God.

Solo 1: He was in the beginning with God.

Solo 2: All things came into being through him, and without him not one thing came into being.

Group 1: What has come into being in him was life,

Group 2: and the life was the light of all people.

Group 1: The light shines in the darkness,

Group 2: and the darkness did not overcome it.

Solo 3: There was a man sent from God, whose name was John.

Solo 4: He came as a witness to testify to the light, so that all might believe through him.

Group 1: He himself was not the light, but he came to testify to the light.

Group 2: The true light, which enlightens everyone, was coming into the world.

All: He was in the world, and the world came into being through him;

Solo 1: yet the world did not know him.

Solo 2: He came to what was his own,

Solo 3: and his own people did not accept him.

Group 2: But to all who received him,

Group 1: who believed in his name,

All: he gave power to become children of God,

Group 1: who were born, not of blood

Group 2: or of the will of the flesh

Group 1: or of the will of man,

All: but of God.

Group 2: And the Word became flesh and lived among us,

Group 1: and we have seen his glory,

Group 2: the glory as of a father's only son,

All: full of grace and truth.

Solo 4: John testified to him and cried out,

Solo 1: "This was he of whom I said, 'He who comes after me
ranks ahead of me because he was before me.'"

All: From his fullness we have all received, grace upon grace.

ELIZABETH AND MARY
by Judith Jolly
Based on Luke 1:5-64

Scene 1

Characters:
Narrator
Zechariah
People outside of the
  Temple
Gabriel

Props:
candle on altar table
  for Temple light
prayer shawl (towel or cloth)
  for men
scarves (towel or cloth)
  for women
tinsel halo for Gabriel

Setting: at the Temple

Narrator: Long ago, in the days of King Herod, there lived a priest whose name was Zechariah. Zechariah was a God-fearing man. Zechariah kept all of God's commandments. Zechariah was married to a woman named Elizabeth. Every day, Zechariah and Elizabeth prayed for a child. But, they did not have any children.

Zechariah: *(lighting the light in the Temple)* Hear, O Israel: The Lord our God is one Lord. You shall love the Lord your God with all your heart, and with all your soul, and with all your might.

Narrator: As Zechariah lit the Temple light, the people outside the Temple prayed.

People outside of the Temple: *(some with hands folded in prayer, some with arms lifted in prayer)* God, hear our prayers!

6

Narrator: Suddenly, Gabriel, an angel of the Lord, appeared beside the altar.

Gabriel: Do not be afraid, Zechariah. God has heard your prayers. You and Elizabeth will have a son. You will name your son John. John will bring you much joy. John will be filled with the Holy Spirit. John will prepare God's people.

Zechariah: *(puzzled)* How can that be? I am old. My wife, Elizabeth, is old. How can we have a baby?

Gabriel: Why do you question me? God sent me to bring you this good news. Because you did not believe, you will not be able to speak until John is born.

People outside of the Temple: What's wrong with Zechariah? Why can't he speak?

Narrator: And Zechariah went home unable to speak.

Scene 2

Characters:
Narrator
Mary
Gabriel

Props:
chair
scarf (towel or cloth)
    for Mary
tinsel halo for Gabriel

Setting: Mary's house

Narrator: The angel Gabriel made another visit. This time Gabriel went to visit a young woman in Nazareth. The young woman's name was Mary. Mary was going to be married to a man named Joseph.

(Mary is seated on a chair. Gabriel stands beside Mary. Mary looks surprised and afraid.)

Gabriel: Do not be afraid, Mary. Peace be with you. God loves you. God has chosen you to do something special for God.

Mary: *(looking puzzled)* What? What do you mean?

Gabriel: Do not be afraid. You will give birth to a son. You will name your son Jesus. Jesus will be called the Son of God. Jesus will be a king.

Mary: How can that be?

Gabriel: Jesus will be God's Son. And I have more good news. Your cousin Elizabeth is also going to have a baby. God can do anything.

Mary: *(smiling)* I will do whatever God asks of me.

Narrator: And the angel Gabriel left Mary.

Scene 3

Characters:
Narrator
Mary
Elizabeth

Props:
scarves (towel or cloth)
  for Mary and Elizabeth
two chairs

Setting: Elizabeth's house

Narrator: Soon after Gabriel visited Mary, Mary got ready to go visit her cousin.

(Elizabeth is sitting on a chair, looking into the distance.)

Mary: *(walking toward Elizabeth)* Hello, Elizabeth! How are you feeling?

Elizabeth: *(standing to hug Mary)* Oh, Mary! I am so glad to see you. Come and sit beside me.

(Mary sits down beside Elizabeth.)

Elizabeth: Even my baby, John, is excited that you are here. You are the most special woman of all. I am honored that you would come to visit with me. I am honored that the mother of the Son of God would come to stay in my home. Seeing you, I know that God's message to you will come true, just like Gabriel said it would.

Mary: *(smiling)* My heart praises God all day long. God is my Savior. I am happy because God has remembered me. I am God's servant. God's name is holy. God shows mercy to all people who honor God. God has brought down mighty kings. God has lifted up the poor and lowly. God has given the poor all that they need. God has kept the promises that God made to our ancestors. God has helped our people. God has shown mercy to us. God will show mercy to our children and to our children's children.

Elizabeth: *(nodding)* Yes, Mary, God is so good. Now, can you stay with me for a little while, Mary?

Mary: *(taking Elizabeth's hand)* I will be happy to stay with you for a few months, Elizabeth.

Narrator: Mary visited with Elizabeth and Zechariah for three months. Then Mary returned to her own home. When John was born, Zechariah spoke again. Zechariah went about praising God.

THE TRIP TO BETHLEHEM

by Judy Newman-St. John
Based on Luke 2:1-5

Characters:
Narrator
Joseph
Mary

Props:
scarf (towel or cloth)
  for Mary
towel or cloth for Joseph

Setting: road to Jerusalem and inside the city

Sound Effects: Have young children pat their legs to make a clip-clop sound.

Narrator: Mary and Joseph are on their way to Bethlehem to be registered. Both are lost in thought as they journey along. Mary is riding a donkey that clip-clops down the rocky dirt road.

(Clip, clop, clip, clop, clip, clop)

Joseph: *(to Mary)* How are you, Mary? Are you tired?

Mary: *(nods yes to Joseph)* Yes, I am. But I think you may be tired as well. Even our little donkey must be tired. He has carried me such a long way.

(Clip, clop, clip, clop, clip, clop)

Joseph: *(to himself)* Yes, I'm tired, and I'm worried. I have more to worry about than paying taxes. I'm sure the governor wants everyone to be registered so he can be certain to get every bit of money he can. I'll register, and I'll pay my taxes. I just hope this trip isn't too hard on Mary. Her baby could come any minute! Hmmm. Her baby? Our baby!

Narrator: Joseph began to remember back to when Mary told him about the angel who had spoken to her. She had felt God's spirit, and she would have a baby, God's Son.

Joseph: *(to himself)* Yes, our baby. I know that he is the Son of God, and I will be his father on earth. Mary and I will love him as much as or even more than any parents ever loved their baby. I will be a good father. I will teach him the Torah, and he will grow up to be a man of God. I will teach him everything I know about woodworking.

(Mary touches Joseph's arm.)

Mary: Joseph, I think I see the city in the distance! I am so glad. I would like to get off of this donkey and rest.

Narrator: Mary was more than willing to go on the long journey with Joseph to his hometown to be registered. The journey was not an easy one, especially for a woman about to have a baby. The little donkey did the best he could to make her trip comfortable. He stepped around rocks and over any rough spots in the road.

(Clip, clop, clip, clop, clip, clop)

Mary: *(to herself)* I know God will take care of us. God sent an angel to Joseph in a dream. The angel told him that my baby is God's beloved child. The angel told Joseph to marry me. And now we are on our way and our baby will be born soon. I will be a good mother to our baby. I will be sure that he is fed and warm and happy. I will take extra care to raise God's chosen child in the way God wants me to.

Mary: *(to Joseph)* I have been thinking about our baby, Jesus. The angel told us to name him Jesus.

Joseph: *(to Mary, smiling)* I have been thinking of Jesus also. I think Jesus is a perfect name for him. I have been wondering if he will look like you.

11

Mary: *(smiling)* He will be beautiful, I know.

Narrator: The couple approached the busy, crowded city. Joseph made his way from inn to inn in search of a place to stay. The little donkey was careful that he did not bump into any person or other animal.

(Clip, clop, clip, clop, clip, clop)

Joseph: Mary, I don't know what to say. All of the inns are full. I must find a place for you to rest.

Narrator: One kind innkeeper offered his stable to Mary and Joseph. It was a place where animals slept, but they could rest there and be warm and dry. Once inside the stable, Joseph made Mary a bed of soft hay.

Joseph: *(to Mary)* Come, my love. Rest a while.

Mary: Yes, I will rest. Soon, very soon, our baby will be born.

PRAISE GOD! JESUS IS BORN!
by LeeDell Stickler and Judy Newman-St. John
Based on Luke 2:1-20

Directions: Have an adult or older child read the story. Assign parts for children to help in the story. You might need to point to the sound effects at the appropriate parts of the story.

You will need these parts:
trumpets: with fists to mouth, make a trumpet sound
donkey hooves: with cupped hands, pat right and left knees
        alternately
crowd: with cupped hands to mouth, repeat the phrase "peas
        and carrots" over and over again
door sounds: knock on a piece of wood or a wooden table or a
        book
animals in the stable: variety of animal sounds (cow, sheep,
        donkey, rooster, mouse, dove)
Chorus: all children to say "Praise God! Jesus is born!"

[Trumpet sounds]
Give ear! Give ear! By order of the Emperor Augustus, all men will go to their home town to be registered.
[Trumpet sounds]

And so Joseph went from Nazareth in Galilee to Judea, to the city of David called Bethlehem, because he was from the house and family of David. And he took with him Mary, who was expecting a child.

[Donkey hooves]
Up the hills and down the hills, the little donkey walked. **[Donkey hooves speed up and then slow down and speed up again.]** The sun was going down. Soon it would be night. **[Donkey hooves slower.]** Mary was tried. Joseph was tired. And the little donkey was even more tired. **[Donkey hooves even slower.]**

When the three came to the little town of Bethlehem, there was quite a crowd. **[Crowd sounds]** In fact, the city was so crowded that there was no place to stay.

Joseph went from house to house. **[Donkey hooves]** He was looking for some place—any place—to stay where Mary could rest and have shelter. There was not an inch of floor space to be found anywhere. Finally Joseph came to an inn. He knocked on the door. **[Door sounds]** The innkeeper opened the door. **[Crowd sounds]**

"Go away!" said the innkeeper. "We have no room tonight!"

Joseph turned to go, pulling the little donkey behind him. **[Donkey hooves]** The innkeeper saw Mary and the tired little donkey. He felt sorry for them.

"Wait, I have no room inside the inn. But I do have a stable where travelers keep their animals. You may sleep there tonight if you'd like," he said.

Joseph looked at Mary wondering how he would feel about sleeping where the animals slept. Mary looked at Joseph and nodded her head yes. Joseph turned back to the innkeeper and nodded.

"Let me show you the way," the kind innkeeper offered. **[Donkey hooves]** "The stable is just over here." The innkeeper led Joseph and Mary and the little donkey to the small stable.

The three looked around. It wasn't much, but there would be a roof over them tonight. And the animals would keep them company. **[Animal sounds]**

Joseph lit a small clay lamp to provide them light. He laid his cloak across the hay. Mary lay down on the soft hay to rest. It had been a long journey. **[Animal sounds]**

Joseph led the little donkey to hay to eat and water to drink. **[Donkey hooves]** Then he took the bundles from the donkey's back and put them close to Mary.

And that night, that very night, with only Joseph and the animals to keep her company, **[soft animal sounds]** Mary gave birth to baby Jesus. She wrapped him in bands of cloth and laid him in a manger where the animals ate.

In that region there were shepherds in the fields, keeping watch over their flock. The angel of the Lord appeared to them and told them good news of great joy. **[Chorus: Praise God! Jesus is born!]** The angel told the shepherds they would find the child wrapped in bands of cloth and lying in a manger. **[Chorus: Praise God! Jesus is born!]** The shepherds hurried and found the child in the stable, just as the angel had told them. They told everyone about the child. **[Chorus: Praise God! Jesus is born!]** The shepherds returned to the field glorifying and praising God for all they had seen and heard. **[Chorus: Praise God! Jesus is born!]**

Baby Jesus, God's greatest gift to the world, was born to save us. **[Chorus: Praise God! Jesus is born!]** Baby Jesus, the Son of God, was born to show us the way. **[Chorus: Praise God! Jesus is born!] [Repeat Chorus: Praise God! Jesus is born!]**

ONCE UPON A STARRY NIGHT
by Judith Jolly
Based on Luke 2:8-15

Characters:
Narrator
Sheep
Benjamin
Aaron
Bright Light
Shepherds
Grandfather
Angel of the Lord
Host of Angels

Props:
towels or pieces of cloth for
  shepherds' cloaks
flashlight for Bright Light to
  turn on

Setting: a shepherds' field out in the country

(Sheep grazing. Shepherds watching.)

Narrator: Once upon a starry night, shepherds carefully watched their sheep. The wind gently stirred the grass. The only sounds the shepherds heard were the sheep grazing around them. Two shepherd boys lay quietly beside their sheep watching the night-time sky. Their grandfather was nearby, resting from the long day's work.

Sheep: Baa! Baa!

Benjamin: Aaron! Aaron! Are you awake?

Aaron: *(yawning)* Of course I'm awake, Benjamin. I am sleepy, though. How about you?

Benjamin: *(stretching and yawning)* I'm sleepy, too. And I'm a little bit chilly. But I am so glad that Grandfather allowed us to come to the field tonight.

16

Aaron: I'm happy to be here, too. *(Aaron sits up.)* Do you think we will see a wolf tonight?

Benjamin: *(sitting up)* Oh, Aaron. Who knows? We will all stay awake to keep our sheep safe.

Sheep: Baa! Baa!

Narrator: Suddenly a huge, bright light appeared!

(Bright Light turns on flashlight.)

Shepherds: *(together)* Look at that light! Look at that light!

Benjamin: Aaron! Aaron! Look at that light! What can it be?

Aaron: Wow! Have you ever seen such a bright light?

(Angel of the Lord stands in the middle of the shepherds.)

Aaron: Oh! Who's that? I'm frightened.

Grandfather: *(as if he is just waking up)* What is it?

(Shepherds look afraid and point toward the Angel of the Lord.)

Angel of the Lord: Do not be afraid. I am bringing you good news. Everyone will be happy when they hear this good news. There will be joy throughout the land. Today, this very day, in the town of Bethlehem, a Savior has been born.

Benjamin: *(whispering)* Can you believe it, Aaron? I wonder if we will find the Savior? I wonder where he is?

Angel of the Lord: You will find this special baby in a stable. This special baby will be lying in a manger. This special baby will be lying on a bed of hay. This special baby will be wrapped in soft cloths.

17

Aaron: Oh, Benjamin! How exciting! Benjamin, look!

(Both boys look up toward the sky.)

Narrator: Suddenly, the skies were filled with angels.

(Host of Angels stand with the shepherds.)

Host of Angels: Glory to God in the highest! Peace on earth to all!

Narrator: And, just as suddenly as they appeared, the angels and the Bright Light were gone. The sky was dark again.

(Bright Light turns off flashlight.)

Grandfather: *(standing)* Come, Aaron and Benjamin. Come with me. Hurry! We are going to Bethlehem. We are going to find this special baby.

Benjamin: I am so excited. Let's walk as fast as we can. Let's go find this special baby.

Aaron: I can hardly wait to see this special baby. Hurry, Benjamin. We will never forget this night.

Benjamin and Aaron: *(together)* Hurry! Hurry, Grandfather!

(Shepherds, sheep, Benjamin, Aaron, and Grandfather walk together.)

FOLLOW THE STAR

by Judith Jolly
Based on Luke 2:8-20

Reader: Shepherds watched their sheep on that starry night.
Girls: Follow, follow, follow the star.

Reader: Suddenly, an angel appeared, lighting the nighttime sky.
Boys: Follow, follow, follow the star.

Reader: The dark night became as bright as day.
Girls: Follow, follow, follow the star.

Reader: The shepherds were filled with fear.
Boys: Follow, follow, follow the star.

Reader: The angel told the shepherds, "Do not be afraid."
Girls: Follow, follow, follow the star.

Reader: "I bring you good news," the angel said.
Boys: Follow, follow, follow the star.

Reader: "Your Savior is born in Bethlehem."
Girls: Follow, follow, follow the star.

Reader: All the angels sang, "Glory to God in the highest."
Boys: Follow, follow, follow the star.

Reader: The shepherds found Mary, Joseph, and the tiny baby.
All: Follow, follow, follow the star.

Reader: The baby was asleep in a manger filled with hay.
All: Follow, follow, follow the star.

Reader: The shepherds returned to their fields praising God.
All: Follow, follow, follow the star.

GLORY TO GOD

by Judith Jolly
Based on Luke 2:8-15 and Matthew 2:11

Characters:
Mary
Joseph
chorus
angel
1st shepherd
2nd shepherd
3rd shepherd
sheep
cows
1st Wise Man
2nd Wise Man
3rd Wise Man

Props:
manger for baby Jesus
doll (Jesus)
crowns for wise men
towels/cloth for shepherds'
  cloaks
towel/cloth for Mary's
  headpiece
towel/cloth for Joseph's cloak
tinsel for angel's halo
2 chairs

Scene 1: a Jewish home

Mary: I talked with an angel today.

Joseph: I talked with an angel, too.

Mary: *(smiling)* I am going to have a baby.

Joseph: That is what the angel told me, too.

Mary: We will name our baby Jesus, just like the angel said.

Chorus: Glory to God in the highest.

Scene 2: a hillside

(Sheep are grazing and shepherds are watching.)

1st Shepherd: What is that bright light?

Angel: Do not be afraid.

2nd Shepherd: What do you mean? What do you want?

Angel: I have good news. A new king is born.

3rd Shepherd: Where is this new king?

Angel: You will find this baby king in Bethlehem.

Chorus: Glory to God in the highest.

Scene 3: a place where animals live

(Sheep and cows stand watching. Mary and Joseph sit beside the manger looking at the baby Jesus.)

Sheep: Baa! Baa!

Cows: Moo! Moo!

Mary: *(smiling)* Oh, Joseph! Our baby is just beautiful!

Joseph: Jesus is a special baby, Mary. God is so good!

(Shepherds and sheep walk toward Mary, Joseph, and the baby Jesus.)

1st, 2nd, and 3rd Shepherds: We have come to see the baby.

Sheep: Baa! Baa!

Cows: Moo! Moo!

Chorus: Glory to God in the highest.

Scene 4: a house

(Wise men walk toward Mary and baby Jesus.)

1st Wise Man: I have brought gold to the baby.

2nd Wise Man: I have brought frankincense to the baby.

3rd Wise Man: I have brought myrrh to the baby.

Mary: Thank you for your gifts. I will remember you always. I will treasure your gifts in my heart forever.

Chorus: Glory to God in the highest!

JUST A LITTLE
by Judith Jolly

Just a little star
Became a brilliant light
Shining on shepherd boys
On a chilly winter's night.

Just a little breeze
On that hillside far away
Sounds of angels singing
Called to shepherds on that day.

Just a little lamb
Grazing on the hill
Went to see the Christ child
In a manger. Oh, so still!

Just a little child
In a manger filled with hay
Showing us God's love
On that first Christmas day.

WISE MEN FOLLOW THE STAR
by Judith Jolly
Based on Matthew 2:1-12

Scene 1

Characters:	Props:
First Wise Man	three crowns
Second Wise Man	
Third Wise Man	

Setting: a room in the East

(Three wise men are gathered, looking up to the sky.)

First Wise Man: The star seems to be brighter tonight.

Second Wise Man: We have watched this star for so long. Now it seems to be moving.

Third Wise Man: Let's follow it. Let's go to see the King. Let's see if King Herod knows anything about the star. If the star really can lead us to the new king, surely King Herod will know how to find the king.

First Wise Man: Surely King Herod has seen the star.

(Wise men walk off together, still looking at the sky.)

Scene 2

Characters:	Props:
First Wise Man	three crowns
Second Wise Man	crown for King Herod
Third Wise Man	chair to be King Herod's
King Herod	throne

Setting: King Herod's throne room

(King Herod sits on his throne.
Wise men walk toward King Herod.)

Second Wise Man: *(kneeling)* O King Herod, have you seen that big star in the sky? Do you know where we can find this King of the Jews?

Third Wise Man: *(kneeling)* O King Herod, we have watched this new star for a long time. Now it is moving. The new star is brighter than ever. Something wonderful is happening.

First Wise Man: *(kneeling)* O King Herod, we have heard that this new star announces a new king. We have heard that a baby king has been born.

King Herod: You may rise! Tell me more.

Third Wise Man: *(standing)* We have traveled a long way. We have watched the star as it has moved across the sky. It seems to have stopped.

Second Wise Man: *(standing)* We want to worship this new king.

First Wise Man: *(standing)* Please help us find the new king.

King Herod: *(angrily)* I cannot believe this! A new king, indeed! Call the chief priests. Call the teachers. Who is this new king?

First Wise Man: We understand that the new king is just a baby.

King Herod: Where is this baby? Why did I not know about this new king? Go! Go, quickly. Find out where this king is. Then, come back to me. Tell me everything that you learn about the new king. I must know where he is.

Second Wise Man: The prophets of long ago wrote about this baby, O King Herod. The Jewish people have waited for many, many years for this king.

Third Wise Man: This baby will be the King of the Jews. He will be the Messiah.

First Wise Man: The Messiah will lead the Jewish people. The Messiah will guide the people of Israel.

King Herod: *(whispering)* Tell me everything. Tell me exactly when the star first appeared. Tell me everything! *(pointing toward the exit)* Now, go! Go quickly. Find this child. When you find the new king, let me know. I want to know where the king is. I want to worship this King of the Jews also. Now, go!

(Wise men leave.)

Scene 3

Characters: **Props:**
First Wise Man   three crowns
Second Wise Man
Third Wise Man

Setting: outside King Herod's palace

(Wise men are walking as they talk.)

Third Wise Man: King Herod had lots of questions.

Second Wise Man: King Herod sounded worried.

First Wise Man: Look! There is the star again!

Second Wise Man: Is it the same star?

Third Wise Man: Oh, yes! It is the same star. It's the star that we saw in the East. I am so glad. This bright star will lead us again.

First Wise Man: *(smiling)* Let's follow the star again.

Second Wise Man: *(smiling)* Let's find this new king.

Third Wise Man: *(smiling)* Let's go find the baby king.

(Wise men continue to walk.)

First Wise Man: *(pointing up toward the sky)* Oh, friends! Look!

Second Wise Man: *(pointing up toward the sky)* The star has stopped!

Third Wise Man: *(pointing up toward the sky)* Look! The star has stopped!

First, Second, Third Wise Men: *(together)* Let's find this baby, this new king!

Scene 4

Characters:	**Props:**
First Wise Man	three crowns
Second Wise Man	three gift-wrapped boxes
Third Wise Man	doll to be baby Jesus
Mary	chair for Mary
	scarf (towel or cloth) for Mary

Setting: a house

(Mary is sitting in a chair, holding baby Jesus.)

First Wise Man: *(kneeling)* Oh! How beautiful! What a beautiful baby!

27

Second Wise Man: *(kneeling)* Oh! He really is the King!

Third Wise Man: *(kneeling)* Oh! I have never felt such joy!

First Wise Man: *(still kneeling)* We have watched a special star for many years.

Second Wise Man: *(still kneeling)* The special star led us to you.

Third Wise Man: *(still kneeling)* The special star stopped just about at this stable.

First, Second, and Third Wise Men: *(together)* And we found the King!

Mary: *(smiling)* Welcome, friends! The baby's name is Jesus!

(Wise men hold out gifts for the baby Jesus.)

First Wise Man: I bring gold to the King.

Second Wise Man: I bring frankincense to the King.

Third Wise Man: I bring myrrh to the King.

Mary: *(smiling)* Your gifts bring honor to our baby.

First, Second, and Third Wise Men: *(together)* We praise the new King! We worship the Messiah!

First Wise Man: *(standing)* We must return to our homes.

Second Wise Man: *(standing)* What a joy it is to see this baby!

Third Wise Man: *(standing)* What a joy it is to see the King!

First, Second, and Third Wise Men: *(together)* Goodbye!

(Wise men leave Mary and the baby.)

Scene 5

Characters:
First Wise Man
Second Wise Man
Third Wise Man

Props:
three crowns

Setting: outside the house

Second Wise Man: I had a dream last night. In my dream, God told me to go home a different way. God told me not to go back to see King Herod.

Third Wise Man: I had a similar dream. God told me that we should not go back to King Herod.

First Wise Man: I agree. I dreamed the same thing.

Second Wise Man: Then, it's decided. We will go home. We will not tell King Herod about the beautiful baby that we saw. We will not tell King Herod about this new King.

First, Second, and Third Wise Men: *(together)* What a glorious sight! What a beautiful baby! What a glorious King!

THE nOT-SO-SILENT nIGHT

by LeeDell Stickler

Based on Luke 2:1-7

Characters:
Angel Chorus
Innkeeper
Grumpy Cow
Dove
Sheep
Mouse
Cat
Owl
Donkey
Mary and Joseph (non-
     speaking parts)

Props:
doll to be Jesus
box to be trough
boxes to be hay bales
optional: straw

Setting:

A stable outside an inn in the little city of Bethlehem. It is nearing the evening. A cow and a sheep are standing in the center. A dove is sitting on a hay bale to the right of the cow and sheep. An owl is sitting on a hay bale to the left of the cow and sheep.

Angel Chorus: Sings "Prepare the Way of the Lord" [*United Methodist Hymnal* #207]

Innkeeper: *(putting fresh straw in the manger)* Here you go, old girl. Dinner time. I know I'm late, but it's been very busy today, with all the people in the town. Would you believe every last space is filled?

Grumpy Cow: *(Sighs)* Last again. I just wish he'd get his priorities straight. I've got needs. I'm a growing girl. Food is very important to me. It's not like I can run down to the marketplace and get the food myself.

Dove: That's a frightening thought—you loose in the marketplace. That's scary on so many levels.

Sheep: Yes, and she conveniently forgets that she is not the only animal in this stable.

Dove: And the fact that we're not people. People come first. After all, he is an innkeeper.

Sheep: From what I could see through the crack in the wall, there are a lot of them too. I've never seen it quite so busy.

Mouse: *(scurrying in and hiding behind the hay bale)* Oh, my aching belly. If I eat one more crumb of bread, one more bite of cheese, one more kernel of wheat, I will explode.

Grumpy Cow: Not in my stable please. If you plan to do something like that I'd prefer you go out to the street. They'll never notice out there.

Mouse: Where's your "love your neighbor" attitude?

Grumpy Cow: But you'd make such a mess.

Mouse: Whatever. *(Curls up on a pile of straw and proceeds to snore.)*

Cat: *(slinking in)* Finally, a warm place to nap! And far away from all those feet!

Mouse: *(Sits up with a start)* Eek!

Cat: Chill. I'm too tired to chase you right now. I've spent all day just avoiding all those feet. If one more person stepped on my tail or kicked me out of the way, I was going to have a hissy fit, right there in the street.

Dove: That's another frightening thought I didn't need.

Mouse: Pardon me if I don't trust that cat entirely. *(moves to another part of stable)* I think I'll curl up over here and get a few winks. I'm so full I couldn't run even if I had to. So I hope someone is keeping watch.

Grumpy Cow: That's right. Come on in. Both of you. Just make yourself at home. Who invited you two? Now, I'll have to watch where I put my feet. If it's not one thing, it's something else. Hrumph.

Angel Chorus: Sings "O Little Town of Bethlehem" (stanza 1) [*United Methodist Hymnal* #230]

Grumpy Cow: Finally. The sun's going down. Maybe everything will quiet down now too. My favorite time. Everyone has gone to sleep. The stable is quiet. Not a thing to disturb me.

Sheep: Disturb you from doing what? Chewing your cud? Eating your hay? Stamping on the dirt floor? It's not like you've got anything better to do.

Grumpy Cow: Hrumph. Even a cow has the right to a little peace and quiet now and then.

Sheep: I'll have to admit, it has been rather noisy around here today.

Owl: Whooooo?

Dove: All those people, that's who. I've never seen Bethlehem so busy. I overheard a few of them talking as they pushed through the crowd. They kept muttering something about taxes and Romans and soldiers. I'm glad I'm not a people. They were not happy.

Owl: Whooo?

Dove: All those people who have come to Bethlehem to register. Following the emperor's new decree.

Owl: Whooo?

Dove: The emperor of Rome. Told everyone they had to go to their home towns to register. More taxes probably.

Owl: Whooo?

Dove: All those people here. The Romans are taxing them to death.

Owl: Whooo?

Dove: Never mind.

Sheep: What did you say about peace and quiet?

Grumpy Cow: Hrumph.

Angel Chorus: Sings "It Came Upon the Midnight Clear" (stanza 1) [*United Methodist Hymnal* #218]

Grumpy Cow: Sheep, are you asleep?

Sheep: I was, but I'm not now. What's the matter?

Grumpy Cow: Something's not right.

Sheep: Oh for crying out loud, you worry too much.

Grumpy Cow: But don't you hear it? Footsteps. Coming right toward the stable. And light—more than there should be at this time of day.

Sheep: Now that you mention it, I do hear someone. It sounds like the innkeeper.

Grumpy Cow: Just what we need, more interruptions. It's the middle of the night! It's time for people to sleep—so it'll be quiet. I need my sleep.

Sheep: It would be a whole lot quieter if you'd just stop talking!

Innkeeper: *(leading the donkey)* Here you go, fellow. There's some fresh hay for you. Now you can rest. You've had a long trip. Right this way. *(Mary and Joseph enter the stable.)* It's not much, but it's the best I can do. Anyway, it's warm. You'll be out of the weather.

Grumpy Cow: Give me a break. More people—and in MY stable, too. Just one more interruption.

Sheep: Get over it, Grumpy. It's just two people and they look so tired. I don't think they are going to make much noise tonight.

Owl: Whooo?

Dove: The man and woman the innkeeper just brought to the stable.

Owl: Whooo?

Dove: I don't know who they are. They just arrived—with the donkey.

Owl: Whoooo?

Dove: Never mind. Why don't you go out hunting field mice or squirrels or something.

Mouse: Now just a minute! He doesn't need any encouragement.

Grumpy Cow: Would everyone please be quiet! I'm trying to get some sleep!

All Animals but Grumpy: Whatever!

Angel Chorus: Sings "Away in a Manger" (stanzas 1-2) [*United Methodist Hymnal* #217]

(Sound of a baby crying.)

Grumpy Cow: Now what? Just when I was sleeping so well.

Donkey: It's a baby, silly.

Grumpy Cow: I know it's a baby. I want to know what it's doing here in my stable.

Sheep: Our stable.

Donkey: I don't think they had a choice. There were no more rooms left in the town.

Grumpy Cow: What do you mean? How do you know?

Donkey: We came all the way from Nazareth. We've been on the road for three days. With the emperor's decree, every room was taken. This was all that was left.

Grumpy Cow: But the woman, she was going to have a baby?

Donkey: That couldn't be helped. Babies don't pay attention to emperors.

Owl: Whoooo?

Dove: Caesar, Caesar Augustus!

Owl: Whooo?

Dove: The one who made the law!

Owl: Whoooo?

Dove: Never mind.

Angel Chorus: Sings "There's a Song in the Air" (stanzas 1-2) [*United Methodist Hymnal* #249]

Grumpy Cow: Hrumph!

Sheep: Now what's the problem?

Grumpy Cow: I'm worried. Where's the baby going to sleep? A baby can't sleep on the floor. A baby needs a place warm and soft and protected.

Cat: What did you expect? This is a stable. You know, a place where the animals sleep.

Grumpy Cow: We've got to do something!

Sheep: We? What can we do? We're only animals.

Cat: Speak for yourself. I'm sure if we put our heads together, we could come up with something.

Donkey: I've got an idea. How about the water bucket. The sides are strong and it will hold a baby.

The Cat: That's not very soft or warm. Besides, it's not big enough. Mouse or I could sleep there, but not a baby.

Mouse: How about the straw basket over there in the corner. It should be big enough. And I know it's soft enough. My family had a nest in there last year.

Dove: Ewww!

Cat: It's big enough. And soft enough. But look how flimsy the sides are. Babies wiggle around a lot. We need something stronger than that to protect a baby.

Dove: What about the wooden crate where the doves sleep? It's big enough. And I know it's strong enough.

Cat: It's big enough. It's strong enough. But it's so hard. How can a baby sleep on something that hard?

Grumpy Cow: I've got an idea. They can use my feed trough. It's big enough for a baby. The hay will make a soft warm bed for the baby. And it's strong enough. It's also off the floor so the night wind won't chill the baby.

Sheep: Our feed trough, you mean?

Grumpy Cow: OK. *Our* feed trough.

Cat: What a great idea, Cow. Are you sure you want to give up your trough for the night?

Grumpy Cow: Hey, it's not always about me. Besides, I'm getting a little round about the middle. I can go without food for one night, anyway.

*(Mary places baby Jesus in the feed trough.
Joseph stands beside her.)*

Angel Chorus: Softly sings "That Boy-Child of Mary" (stanzas 1–6) [*United Methodist Hymnal* #241]

Grumpy Cow: All right now, everyone, let's quiet down. It's late. Everyone should be asleep. No moving. No scurrying. No stamping. There's a baby in here. Quiet.

All the Animals: *(to the cow)* Sssh!

Angel Chorus: Sings "Silent Night" (stanzas 1, 3, 4) [*United Methodist Hymnal* #239]

SOUNDS OF CHRISTMAS

by Judith Jolly
Based on Luke 2:8-20 and Matthew 2:1-12

Reader: Breezes blowing.
Children make blowing sound, like blowing out candles.

Reader: Shepherds watching.
Children shade eyes with hand, looking off in the distance.

Reader: Stars twinkling.
Children sing "Twinkle, Twinkle Little Star."

Reader: Sheep grazing.
Children: Baa! Baa!

Reader: Angels singing.
Children: Glory to God in the highest!

Reader: Cattle lowing.
Children: Moo! Moo!

Reader: Donkeys eating.
Children: Crunch! Crunch!

Reader: Camels plodding.
Children stomp first one foot, then the other foot.

Reader: Wise men following.
Children point to the sky.

Reader: Wise men giving.
Children hold out arms, offering gifts.

Reader: Joseph smiling.
Children smile broadly.

Reader: Baby crying.
Children: Waa! Waa!

Reader: Mary rocking.
Children sway back and forth.

Reader: Mary singing.
*Children sing "Silent Night," stanza 1 [*United Methodist Hymnal *#239].*

A CHRISTMAS LITANY

by Judith Jolly

With shepherds keeping watch so long ago,
We celebrate the birth of Jesus.

With angels singing, "Glory to God in the highest,"
We celebrate the birth of Jesus.

With that brightest star that led the faithful to Bethlehem,
We celebrate the birth of Jesus.

With the innkeeper who shared the animals' shelter,
We celebrate the birth of Jesus.

With wise men who studied stars and brought gifts,
We celebrate the birth of Jesus.

With Joseph, who lovingly watched over Mary and the child,
We celebrate the birth of Jesus.

With Mary, who mothered the Christ child so long ago,
We celebrate the birth of Jesus.

GETTING READY FOR CHRISTMAS
by Daphna Flegal

Have the children stand in a circle. Sing the song "Getting Ready for Christmas" to the tune of "This Is the Way." Invite the children to do the motions suggested.

This is the way we trim our tree,
(Pretend to hang ornaments on a tree.)
Trim our tree, trim our tree.
This is the way we trim our tree,
Getting ready for Christmas.

This is the way we sing our songs,
(Cup hands around mouth.)
Sing our songs, sing our songs.
This is the way sing our songs,
Getting ready for Christmas.

This is the way we go to church,
(March in place.)
Go to church, go to church.
This is the way we go to church,
Getting ready for Christmas.

This is the way we pray for friends,
(Fold hands in prayer.)
Pray for friends, pray for friends.
This is the way we pray for friends,
Getting ready for Christmas.

MARY'S SONG

(Luke 1:46-55, CEV)

Girls: With all my heart I praise the Lord,

Boys: and I am glad because of God my Savior.

Solo 1: God cares for me, his humble servant.

Solo 2: From now on, all people will say God has blessed me.

Boys: God All-Powerful has done great things for me, and his name is holy.

Girls: He always shows mercy to everyone who worships him.

Solo 1: The Lord has used his powerful arm to scatter those who are proud.

Solo 2: God drags strong rulers from their thrones and puts humble people in places of power.

Solo 1: God gives the hungry good things to eat, and sends the rich away with nothing.

Girls: God helps his servant Israel

Boys: and is always merciful to his people.

All: The Lord made this promise to our ancestors, to Abraham and his family forever!

PRAYERS

Dear God, as we celebrate the days before Christmas, help us to remember your special gift, Jesus. Amen.

Dear God, we thank you for your gift of Jesus. Help us to remember Jesus in everything we do as we prepare to celebrate his birth. Amen.

Thank you, God, for your gift of Jesus. We can share the good news of Jesus' birth with everyone. Amen.

Dear God, we thank you for Jesus, whom you sent to be the Savior of all people everywhere. Amen.

Thank you, God, for your Son, Jesus. Thank you for the hope Jesus brings to our lives today. Amen.

Dear God, thank you for your Son, Jesus. Thank you for the message of love and peace that Jesus gave to all the people. Help us today to live in peace and love with one another. Amen.

Dear God, thank you for sending Jesus, the promised Messiah. People long ago waited for Jesus to save them from their pain and suffering. Thank you for the difference Jesus makes in our lives. Jesus is our loving Savior, who is our example of how we should live. Amen.

Thank you, God, for your Son, Jesus. Thank you for sending him to help us know what you are like. Jesus' birth proves that your love is for all people. Thank you, God, that your love is for me. Amen.

ADVENT CANDLE-LIGHTING SERVICE
by Judith Jolly

The Advent Wreath contains four purple candles and one white candle. The purple candles are placed in a circle (wreath) and surrounded by greenery, either natural or artificial. The white candle, the Christ candle, is placed in the center of the wreath. Beginning with the first Sunday of Advent, a candle is lighted each Sunday. Each Sunday, one additional candle is lighted so that by the Sunday preceding Christmas, all four purple candles are burning brightly. On Christmas Day, all of the candles are lit.

First Sunday of Advent

Reader 1: This is the first Sunday of the church season we call Advent. Advent is a time when we wait and get ready to celebrate the birth of the Savior. The Savior is Jesus.

All: The light from this candle seems to say,
Come, Lord Jesus, come, we pray.

Reader 2: We light the first candle of Advent to remind us that the people in Bible times hoped that God would send the Messiah to bring them good news of God's love. We light the candle of hope.

Child: I light the candle of HOPE.
(Light one purple candle.)

Teacher or older child: The prophet Isaiah said, "The earth and its people are covered with darkness, but the glory of the Lord is shining upon you" (Isaiah 60:2, CEV).

All: Jesus is the HOPE of the world.

Teacher or older child: Thank you, God, for sending Jesus, our Savior. Fill us with hope. Amen.

Second Sunday of Advent

Reader 1: Today is the second Sunday in Advent. This is the second of four Sundays that we prepare for the birth of Jesus.

All: The light from this candle seems to say,
Come, Lord Jesus, come, we pray.

Reader 2: Today, we light the second candle. It is the candle of love. We remember the message of the angel to Mary. We remember that Jesus is God's message of love.

Child: I light the candle of LOVE.
(Light two purple candles.)

Teacher or older child: God loves us so much. God sent God's only Son to live among us. God's son, Jesus, taught us about God's love. The Scriptures tell us, "For God so loved the world that he gave his only Son, so that everyone who believes in him may not perish but may have eternal life" (John 3:16).

All: Jesus is the LOVE of the world.

Teacher or older child: Dear God, help us to remember your most precious love gift to us, Jesus our Savior. Amen.

Third Sunday of Advent

Reader 1: Today is the third Sunday in the season of Advent.

All: The light from this candle seems to say,
Come, Lord Jesus, come, we pray.

Reader 2: Today we light the third candle. We remember the joy that Mary had in her heart as she knew that

God would keep God's promise and baby Jesus would be born soon.

Child: I light the candle of JOY.
(*Light three purple candles.*)

Teacher or older child: The prophet Isaiah tells us, "The people ...will come back singing. ... Happiness will be a crown they will always wear" (Isaiah 35:10, CEV). When Jesus comes, people will be happy forever and forever free from sorrow and grief.

All: Jesus is the JOY of the world.

Teacher or older child: Thank you, God, for Mary and Joseph. Thank you for giving us the greatest gift of love, baby Jesus. Thank you for the joy we feel during this Christmas season. Amen.

Fourth Sunday of Advent

Reader 1: Today is the fourth Sunday of the season of Advent.

All: The light from this candle seems to say,
Come, Lord Jesus, come, we pray.

Reader 2: Today we light the fourth candle. We remember the angel's message to the shepherds of peace to all people on earth.

Child: I light the candle of PEACE.
(*Light all four purple candles.*)

Teacher or older child: We read in the book of Isaiah:
"A child has been born for us,
a son given to us;
authority rests upon his shoulders;
and he is named
Wonderful Counselor, Mighty God,
Everlasting Father, Prince of Peace" (Isaiah 9:6).

All: Jesus is the PEACE of the world.

Teacher or older child: Thank you, God, for your gift of love, baby Jesus, who brings us peace. Help us to remember that we can bring peace to persons in our community. Amen.

Christmas Day

Reader 1: The time of waiting is over. We have been waiting to celebrate the birth of Jesus, and it has finally come.

All: The light from this candle seems to say,
Come, Lord Jesus, come, we pray.

Reader 2: We light again the candles of hope, love, joy, and peace. Today we light the Christ candle. Lord Jesus has come.

Child: I light the candle of CHRIST.
(Light all four purple candles and the white candle.)

Teacher or older child: We read in the Book of Luke the message from the angels, "I am bringing you good news of great joy for all the people: to you is born this day in the city of David a Savior, who is the Messiah, the Lord" (Luke 2:10-11).

All: Lord Jesus has come!

Teacher or older child: Thank you, God, for the gift of Jesus who brings us hope, love, joy, and peace. Amen.

SCRIPTURE INDEX